This book belongs to

....

Palace Statues and Other Stories

How this collection works

This *Biff, Chip and Kipper* collection is one of a series of four books at **Read with Oxford Stage 3**. It is divided into two distinct halves.

The first half focuses on phonics, with two stories written using the phonics that your children will have learned at school: *Craig Saves the Day* and *Change Gear! Steer!* The second half contains two stories that use everyday language: *Arctic Adventure* and *Palace Statues.* These stories help to broaden your child's wider reading experience. There are also fun activities to enjoy throughout the book.

How to use this book

Find a time to read with your child when they are not too tired and are happy to concentrate for about fifteen minutes. Reading at this stage should be a shared and enjoyable experience. It is best to choose just one story for each session.

There are tips for each part of the book to help you make the most of the stories and activities. The tips for reading on pages 4 and 28 show you how to introduce your child to the phonics stories.

The tips for reading on pages 58 and 88 explain how you can best approach reading the stories that use a wider vocabulary. At the end of each of the four stories you will find four 'Talk about the story' questions. These will help your child to think about what they have read, and to relate the story to their own experiences. The questions are followed by a fun activity.

Enjoy sharing the stories!

Contents

Phonics

Stories for Wider Reading

OXFORD
UNIVERSITY PRESS

Phonics

Tips for reading *Craig Saves the Day*

Children learn best when reading is relaxed and enjoyable.

- Talk about the title and the picture on page 5, and read the speech bubble.

- Identify the letter patterns *ai*, *a-e* and *ay* in the title and talk about the sound they make when you read them ('ai').

- Look at the *ai*, *a-e* and *ay* words on page 6. Say the sounds in each word and then say the word (e.g. *w-ai-t, wait; r-a-c-e, race; s-t-ay, stay*).

- Read the story together, then find the words with *ai*, *a-e* and *ay* in them.

- Talk about the story and do the fun activity at the end of the story.

Children enjoy re-reading stories and this helps to build their confidence.

Have fun!

After you have read the story, play Kim's Game on page 14. How many objects can you remember?

The main sound practised in this story is 'ai' as in *Craig, day, game*.

For more activities, free eBooks and practical advice to help your child progress with reading visit **oxfordowl.co.uk**

Craig
Saves the Day

Who will win the games?

Say the sound and read the words

ai

- Gail
- wait
- tails
- Craig

ay

- day
- hooray
- stay
- play

a-e

- ate
- race
- game
- lake

"So this is Haygate Lake,"
said Chip.

Gail was the leader.

"Wait for Craig," she said.

"Let Chip push me," said Craig.

"It's a fun day with games and races," said Gail.

"You stay in the same team
all day," she said.

Wilf, Chip and Craig were in the
red team.

They played a game called 'Tails', but the green team won.

They played 'Kim's Game'. Craig
was good at it.

"Hooray," yelled Chip.

"We won. The red team won."

Craig got all ten!

It was time to eat. Wilf had a cake.

He gave it to Gail and they all
ate some.

They had an egg and spoon race.

The green team won.

They had a pea race and Craig won it.

The last game was a boat race.

Craig won the race.

"Good for Craig," said Chip.

Talk about the story

What was the first game they played?

Why was Chip glad that Craig was in the red team?

Which games was Craig good at?

What games do you like to play?

ai, ay or a–e?

The sound 'ai' can be spelled ai, ay and a–e. Match the right 'ai' spelling to the pictures and complete the word.

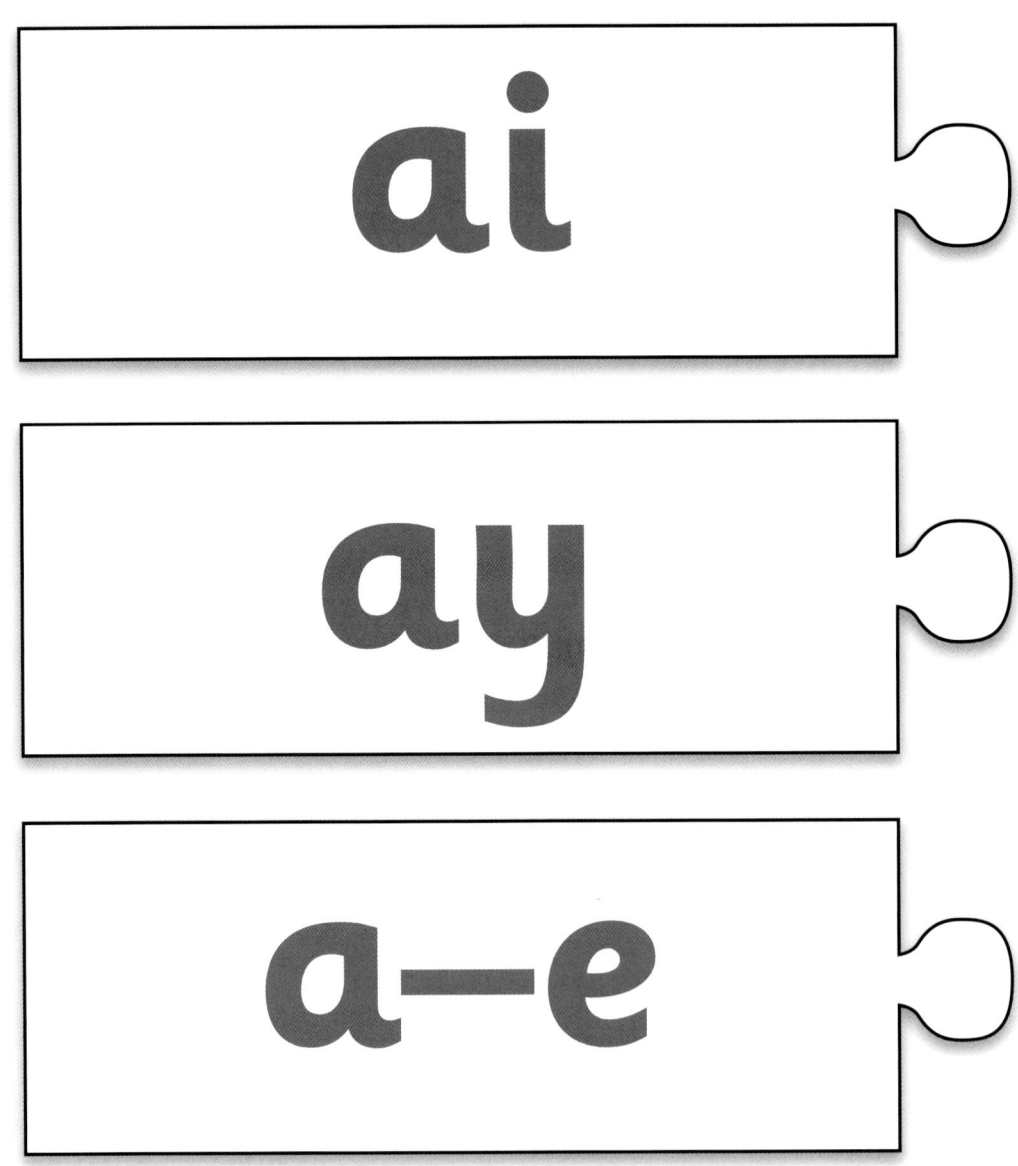

g_m_

r__n

pl__

Cr__g

tr__

g_t_

Picture puzzle

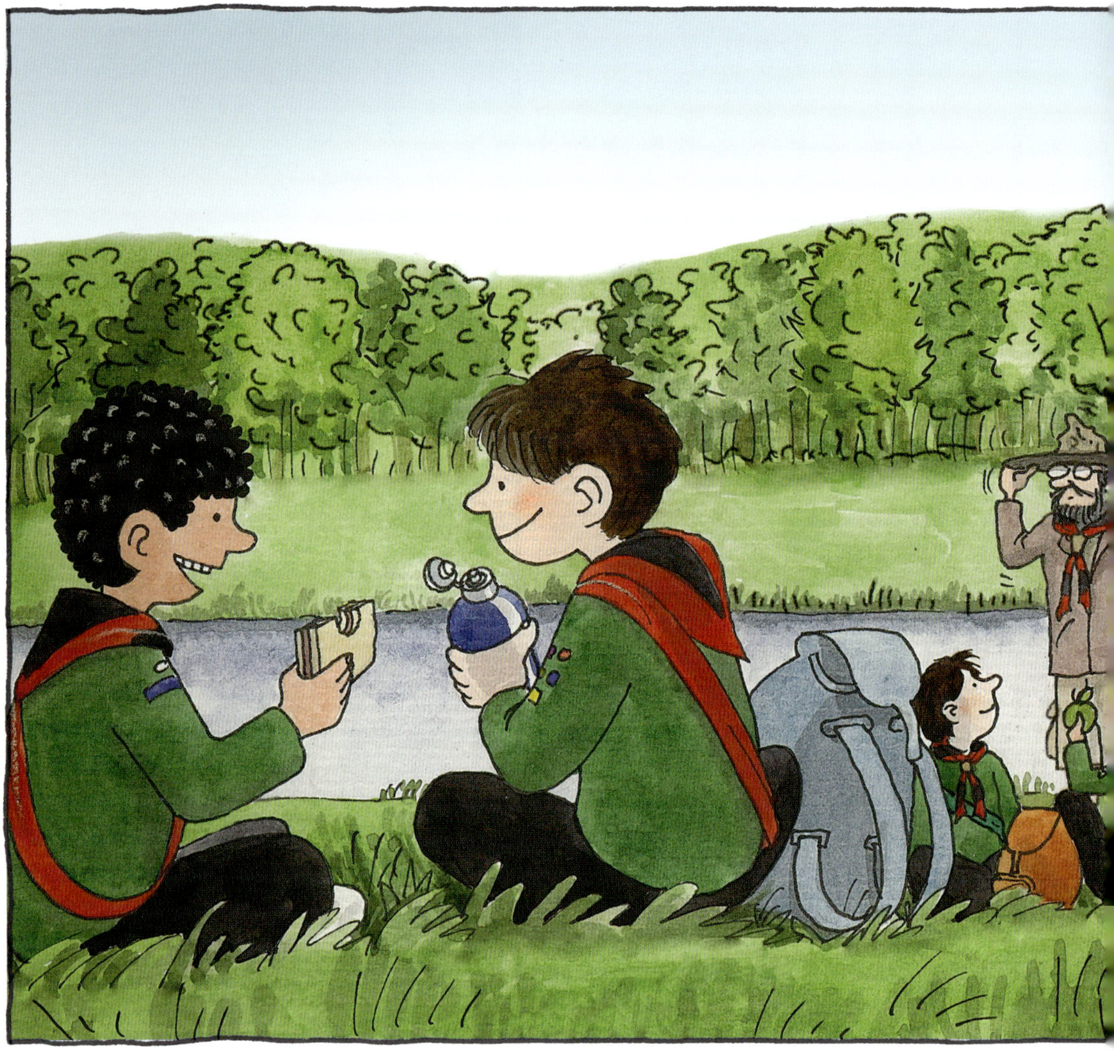

Find as many *ai*, *ay* and *a–e* words as you can in the picture.

ai

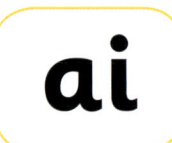

ay

a-e

Tips for reading *Change Gear! Steer!*

Children learn best when reading is relaxed and enjoyable.

- Talk about the title and the picture on page 29, and read the speech bubble.
- Identify the letter patterns *ear* and *eer* in the title and talk about the sound they make when you read them.
- Look at the words on page 30. Say the sounds in each word and then say the word (e.g. *g-ear, h-ere, p-ier, sh-eer*).
- Read the story, then find the words with the letter patterns *ear, ere, eer* and *ier* in them.
- Talk about the story and do the fun activity at the end of the story.

Children enjoy re-reading stories and this helps to build their confidence.

After you have read the story, find the ten seagulls in the pictures.

The main sound practised in this
story is 'ear' as in *near*.

For more activities, free eBooks and practical advice to help your child progress with reading visit **oxfordowl.co.uk**

Change Gear! Steer!

Who will win the car race, Nadim or his Dad?

Read these words

here

veered

nearly

sheer

pier

severe

clear

cheered

Nearly every year Nadim and his dad went to the seaside.

Nadim liked to go to the arcade with his dad. The arcade was on the pier.

"They have really exciting games
in here," said Nadim.

Nadim saw a game called Racing Ace.
"Wow!" said Nadim. "Let's race here."

"Yes, let's race," said Nadim's dad.
"But one thing is clear. I'm an
ace racer."

The screen said ...

Select a car

Nadim chose one with a rear spoiler.

Nadim's dad chose a blue car.

It had three gears like Nadim's.

Nadim could hear a cheer from the crowd.

He gripped the steering wheel.

The light went green.
The screen said ... GO!

"We're off," yelled Nadim's dad.

He shot off so fast that his car spun off at the first bend.

Nadim's car was hard to steer.

It veered to the right but he got past his dad.

The road went up a steep hill. It came to a sharp bend.

"I must not brake too hard," said
Nadim, "in case I spin off like Dad."

The road went down a mountain.
It had a sheer drop on one side.

Nadim slowed down for
another bend.

"Here I come!" yelled Nadim's dad.

Nadim's dad nearly hit the rear of Nadim's car. He shot past but he took the bend too fast.

The car spun round and shot off the road.

"Hard luck, Dad," said Nadim.

The road went into a forest. Nadim came to a clearing. Oh no! It was a dead end.

Nadim had to turn and go back.
"Hard luck, Nadim," said his dad.

The race was almost over, but Nadim just had to get past his dad. He could see the final bend.

Nadim took a risk. He saw a gap and put his foot down. He cut the corner at speed and shot past.

Nadim had won the race.

The crowd cheered.

"Oh dear!" said Nadim's dad. "I
nearly did it. Well done, Nadim."

"Let's come here again," said Nadim.

"Yes, but you won't win next time," said his dad.

Talk about the story

Why did Nadim like going to the arcade on the pier?

Who thought they would win, Nadim or Dad?

Why was Nadim careful not to brake too hard?

What games do you like to play?

Maze

Help Nadim win the car rally and get to the finish line.

FINISH

Stories for Wider Reading

Children learn best when reading is relaxed and enjoyable. These two stories use simple everyday language. You can help your child to read any more challenging words in the context of the story. Children enjoy re-reading stories and this helps to build their confidence and their vocabulary.

Tips for reading *Arctic Adventure*

- Talk about the title and the picture on page 59, and read the speech bubble.

- Share the story, encouraging your child to read as much of it as they can.

- Give lots of praise as your child reads, and help them when necessary.

- If your child gets stuck on a word that is easily decodable, encourage them to say the sounds and then blend them together to read the word. Read the whole sentence again. Focus on the meaning. If the word is not decodable, or is still too tricky, just read the word for them and move on.

- When you've finished reading the story, talk about it with your child, using the 'Talk about the story' questions at the end.

- Do the activity on page 86.

- Re-read the story later, again encouraging your child to read as much of it as they can.

Have fun!

This story includes these useful common words:

clothes   everywhere
glad   soon   suddenly

 For more activities, free eBooks and practical advice to help your child progress with reading visit **oxfordowl.co.uk**

Arctic Adventure!

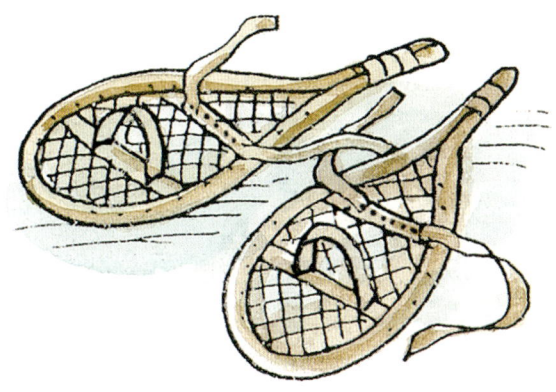

Chip and Wilf have an Arctic adventure!

Wilf was staying with Chip. It was
very hot.

"It's too hot to sleep," said Chip.

"I wish we were in the Arctic," said Wilf. "It's cold there."

Suddenly, the magic key began to glow. It took them into an adventure.

The key took Chip and Wilf to the
Arctic. There was snow everywhere.

The snow felt cold. "Brrrr!" said
Chip. "Now, I'm freezing."

Wilf saw a girl. "Help!" he called.
"We are freezing in this snow."

The girl came over. "You need some warm clothes," she said.

"My name is Oona," said the girl.
"Put these clothes on."

"Now you can help me catch some fish," said Oona.

"You can't catch fish in the snow,"
said Chip.

"I can," said Oona.

There was ice under the snow. Under
the ice was the sea. Oona made a hole
and they started to fish.

Soon, they had five fish.

Suddenly, Chip saw a polar bear.

"Run!" he gasped. "It's going to eat us!"

Chip and Wilf ran.

"It's hard to run in the snow," panted Wilf.

"Stop!" called Oona. "The bear just wants some fish."

"She's only a cub, and she's lost," said
Oona. "I've been helping my dad to
find her."

The cub ate the fish and soon
fell asleep.

"I'll call Dad now," said Oona.

Oona's dad came. "Well done, Oona,"
he said. "Now we can get the cub back
to her mother."

They put the cub on a sled and set
off across the snow.

"The cub needs her mother," said
Oona. "She hasn't learned to hunt yet."

They saw a big polar bear on the ice.
"Is that her mother?" asked Wilf.

The mother bear gave a roar. Then she dived into the sea and swam to her cub.

"I'm glad we helped the cub find her mother," said Oona.

"I'm glad I'm not a polar bear!"
said Chip.

Just then, the key began to glow.

"That was a cold adventure,"
said Wilf.

"But it's still hot!" said Chip.

Talk about the story

How did Oona catch the fish?

Why did the bear cub need her mother?

Why do you think people want to help polar bears?

If you were very hot, how would you cool down? If you were very cold, how would you keep warm?

A maze

Help the mother polar bear find her way to her cub.

Tips for reading *Palace Statues*

Children learn best when reading is relaxed and enjoyable.

- Talk about the title and the picture on page 89, and read the speech bubble.

- Share the story, encouraging your child to read as much of it as they can.

- Give lots of praise as your child reads, and help them when necessary.

- If your child gets stuck on a word that is easily decodable, encourage them to say the sounds and then blend them together to read the word. Read the whole sentence again. Focus on the meaning. If the word is not decodable, or is still too tricky, just read the word for them and move on.

- When you've finished reading the story, talk about it with your child, using the 'Talk about the story' questions at the end.

- Do the activity on page 116.

- Re-read the story later, again encouraging your child to read as much of it as they can.

Have fun!

After you have read the story, find the ten mice hidden in the pictures.

This story includes these useful common words:
called   children   might   suddenly

For more activities, free eBooks and practical advice to help your child progress with reading visit **oxfordowl.co.uk**

Palace Statues

What happened to the palace statues?

The children put on a play called
The Golden Statue. Chip was the
statue. He had on a golden cloak and
gold face paint.

"I like this gold face paint,"
said Anneena.

The magic key began to glow.

The magic took the children to a
palace. They saw a man talking to
a girl.

"Don't cry, Eva," he said.

"What's the matter?" asked Biff.

"This is my brother, Aran," said Eva.
"He guards the golden statues in
the palace."

"The statues all have jewels," said
Aran. "But someone is stealing the
jewels, and I *must* catch the robber."

Aran showed the children the golden statues. "The robber might steal more jewels tonight," he said. "What can I do?"

Chip had an idea. "You can dress up as a golden statue," he said. "Then you can keep watch."

That night, Aran dressed up as a golden statue.

"I'm glad we've got this gold face paint," said Anneena.

Aran went into the statue room. He stood in the deepest shadows. "You need a jewel," said Eva. She gave him her necklace, and went out.

Suddenly, a secret door slid open.
Two men crept into the room. They
took the rest of the jewels.

One of the men spotted Aran.

"I didn't see that statue last night," he said. "Let's get that necklace."

Aran held his breath as the man grabbed the necklace.

At last, he heard a soft thud as the secret door slid shut.

Aran called the
children. He showed
them the secret door. They
all crept down some steps and
along a shadowy tunnel.

Suddenly, Biff tripped and fell.

"Who's there?" shouted the men.

"Run!" whispered Nadim. "Hide under the steps."

A robber came up to the steps. He
held up his lamp but the children were
as still as statues.

"There's nobody here," he said.

The men went into a dusty room.
The children followed them and peeped
round the door.

"There's another door!" said Aran.
"It must lead into the palace garden.
They might escape through that."

"I know what we can do," said
Nadim, and he told the others his plan.
"That's a good idea," said Eva.

Eva raced back up the steps. She told
the guards to go to the garden door.
Then she ran back to the others.

Aran marched stiffly into the dusty room.

"Give me back my necklace!" he roared, in a voice like thunder.

The robbers jumped up.

"Help! The statue is alive!" they screamed. They raced out of the garden door . . .

. . . and ran right into the guards!

The next day, Aran and Eva gave the children a golden statue.

"Thank you for helping us," they said. The magic key began to glow.

The magic took the children home.

"The statue looks just like Eva," said Nadim.

"Yes," said Chip. "And Anneena looks just like the statue!"

Talk about the story

Why was Eva crying?

What was Nadim's plan?

How do you think the children felt when they were hiding?

How would you help someone who was crying?

Picture puzzle

Help Aran to match the jewels to the statues.

Remembering the stories together

Encourage your child to remember and retell the stories in this book. You could ask questions like these:

- Who are the characters?
- What happens at the beginning?
- What happens next?
- How does the story end?
- What was your favourite part? Why?

Story prompts

When talking to your child about the stories, you could use these more detailed reminders to help them remember the exact sequence of events. Turn the statements below into questions, so that your child can give you the answers. For example, *What are the children doing in the story? Why are the children put into teams?* And so on …

Craig Saves the Day

- The children are on a cub trip.
- The children are put into teams to play games and races.
- Wilf, Chip and Craig's team win a game.
- Wilf shares his cake with Gail and the others.
- Craig wins the pea race for the team.
- He then wins the boat race too!

Change Gear! Steer!

- Nadim and his dad are at the seaside and Nadim wants to play a racing game.
- His dad thinks he's going to win.
- His dad spins around too fast and shoots off the road.
- Nadim shoots past his dad and wins the race!

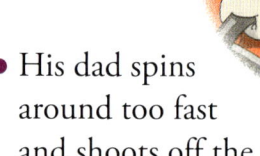

Arctic Adventure

- Wilf and Chip are too hot to sleep.
- The magic key takes Wilf and Chip to the Arctic.
- Oona gives them warm clothes to wear.
- They help Oona to fish.

- Wilf and Chip run from a polar bear cub, but she just wants fish!
- They manage to return the polar bear cub to her mother.

Palace Statues

- The children are putting on a play called *The Golden Statue*.
- The magic key begins to glow and they are taken to a palace.
- Someone is stealing the jewels from all of the statues.
- Chip suggests that Aran dress up as a statue to keep watch.

- Two men creep through a secret door and take the jewels.
- The robbers think the statue is alive and run from Aran straight to the guards!

You could now encourage your child to create a 'story map' of each story, drawing and colouring all the key parts of them. This will help them to identify the main elements of the stories and learn to create their own stories.

Authors and illustrators

Craig Saves the Day written by Roderick Hunt, illustrated by Nick Schon
Change Gear! Steer! written by Roderick Hunt, illustrated by Nick Schon
Arctic Adventure written by Roderick Hunt, illustrated by Alex Brychta
Palace Statues written by Cynthia Rider, illustrated by Alex Brychta

OXFORD
UNIVERSITY PRESS

Great Clarendon Street, Oxford, OX2 6DP, United Kingdom

Oxford University Press is a department of the University
of Oxford. It furthers the University's objective of excellence
in research, scholarship, and education by publishing
worldwide. Oxford is a registered trade mark of Oxford
University Press in the UK and in certain other countries

Arctic Adventure, *Craig Saves the Day*, *Change Gear! Steer!* text © Roderick Hunt 2006, 2008
Palace Statues text © Cynthia Rider 2008

Arctic Adventure, *Palace Statues* illustrations © Alex Brychta 2006, 2008
Craig Saves the Day, *Change Gear! Steer!* illustrations © Alex Brychta and Nick Schon 2008

The characters in this work are the original creation of Roderick Hunt
and Alex Brychta who retain copyright in the characters

The moral rights of the authors have been asserted

Arctic Adventure first published in 2006
Craig Saves the Day, *Change Gear! Steer!*, *Palace Statues* first published in 2008

This Edition published in 2018

British Library Cataloguing in Publication Data
Data available

ISBN: 978-0-19-276426-3

10 9 8 7 6 5 4 3 2

Paper used in the production of this book is a natural, recyclable product
made from wood grown in sustainable forests. The manufacturing process
conforms to the environmental regulations of the country of origin.

Printed in China

Acknowledgements

Series Editors: Annemarie Young and Kate Ruttle